The Highland

Cover picture: Sheep grazing in front of the ruins of a crofting township in Wester Ross.
Inside cover picture: Kylerhea-looking across Sound of Sleat to the mainland.
Title page picture:Loch Bracadale, Isle of Skye.
First published in 1993 by Wayland (Publishers) Ltd,
61 Western Road, Hove, East Sussex BN3 1JD, England.
© Copyright 1993 Wayland (Publishers) Ltd.
British Library Cataloguing in Publication Data

Gunn, Donald
   Highland Clearances
   I.Title II.Spankie, Mari
   333.314115

ISBN 0-7502-0753-1

Consultant: Richard Dargie, Curriculum Development Officer for History, Grampian Region; author of a number of publications on Scottish history.
Editors: Catherine Ellis and Stephen White-Thomson
Concept design: Derek Lee
Book design and typesetting: Pardoe Blacker Limited
Printed and bound by B.P.C.C. Paulton Books, Great Britain

Picture acknowledgements

The publishers would like to thank the following for providing the illustrations: City of Edinburgh Museums & Art Galleries/Bridgeman Art Library, London 11 (Sir Joseph Paton's *At Bay*), 12 (All Hallows Fair by Howe, James 1780-1836); City of York Art Gallery/Bridgeman Art Library 20 (Richard Andsell's *Drovers in Glen Sligichan, Isle of Skye*); Peter Duncan 40, 41 (top); David Gowans 41 (bottom); By courtesy of Edinburgh City Libraries 31 (top); Mary Evans Picture Library 10, 22 (top), 23 (top), 32 (bottom), 37 (left), 38 (bottom), 39; Glasgow Museums: Art Gallery & Museum, Kelvingrove 28 (Thomas Faed's *The Last of the Clan*); Donald Gunn 21 (bottom), 27 (top); Hulton Deutsch Collection 29; Cailean Maclean cover, endpaper, title page, 21 (top), 31 (bottom), 37 (right), 41 (bottom); Mansell 17, 32 (top), 33 (both), 34; Scottish National Portrait Gallery 13 (bottom) (*Sir Murray Mungo*, by John Michael Wright), 18 (*Field Marshall George Wade*, attrib. J. van Diest); Trustees of the National Library of Scotland 16, 25; Trustees of the National Library of Scotland and the Sutherland Estates Office 23 (bottom); Trustees of the National Museums of Scotland 7, 9, 27 (bottom); Photri 36 (top) (J. McCauley); The Royal Collection © 1993 Her Majesty the Queen 19 (David Morier's *A Jacobite Incident: Culloden*), 38 (top) (Carl Haag's *Morning in the Highlands*); Jo Scott/Dunbeath Preservation Trust 30; STB/Still Moving Pic Co 13 (top) (Paul Tomkins), 22 (bottom) (Doug Corrance).
Artwork was supplied by: Sallie Alane Reason 8, 10, 11, 24, 36, 44; Gavin Rowe cover, 6, 25, 26; Mike Taylor cover, 9, 14–15. Thanks to Charles W.J. Withers 1984 *Gaelic in Scotland 1698–1981: The geographical history of a Language* (Edinburgh, John Donald), for the map reference on page 10.

Clearances

Contents

The Ross-shire Sheep Riot

The year was 1792, and the people who lived in the Highlands in the north of Scotland were worried. The land that they had thought of as their own for a thousand years was being taken over by Lowland sheep farmers. The landowners had realized they could make a lot of money from farming a new breed of sheep, the Cheviot. The people who lived in the Highlands, the Gaels, had to go.

During August, a group of Gaels from Ross-shire rose up to defy the new Lowland sheep farmers. They called on others to protest too. Four hundred men met on the banks of the River Oykel. They gathered together as many of the hated sheep as they could find, and drove them off their lands

Around the same time a bloody revolution was taking place in France, in which many landowners were killed.

Sheriff MacLeod of Ross was worried by the Gaels' unrest. He sent for soldiers to help. In London, the government did not want to have a rebellion on its hands, so it ordered the Black Watch (a Highland regiment) to march north from Edinburgh.

David Stewart of Garth, a lieutenant in the 42nd Black Watch regiment, reported on the Ross-shire Sheep Riot:

'No act of violence or outrage occurred, nor did the sheep suffer in the smallest degree . . . Though pressed with hunger, these conscientious peasants did not take a single animal for their own use.'

But when the soldiers reached the Gaels' night camp the men had gone, leaving their peat-fires warm and the sheep asleep.

The Sheriff and his men chased the men of Ross and took their leaders prisoner. On 14 September 1792, five men were tried in Inverness. They were sentenced to imprisonment or transportation (which meant being sent by prison ship to a British Colony overseas). One night, before their sentences were carried out, the men escaped. A large reward was offered for their capture, but they were never heard of again.

It was the end of the Ross-shire Sheep Riot. The men of Ross returned to their glens, and waited to be turned out of their homes. It was clear that the law and the soldiers were not on the people's side.

To understand these events and the story of the Highland Clearances, we need to look back to earlier times in Scotland.

An officer of the Black Watch, 1792.

Who are the Gaels?

The Gaels are the original Scots, and Scotland is named after them. They arrived in Scotland from Ireland about 1,500 years ago. Scotti, or Scots, is the name the Romans used for the Gaels. They settled in many parts of Scotland. We can tell this by looking at the evidence of place names.

Scottish Gaelic is one of the Celtic family of languages. Its roots go back to a time when Celtic speech was widespread in Europe. ('Celtic' is pronounced with a hard 'c', as in 'cat').

Gaelic word	English meaning	Seen on English maps as	Example of place name
achadh	field	auch/ach/auquh	**Auch**inleck
baile	farming village	bal	**Bal**erno
ceann	head	kin/ken	**Kin**ross
cill	church	kil/keil	**Kil**marnock
druim	hill ridge	drum	Oldmel**drum**
dun	fort	dun/dum/doon	**Dun**bar
inbhir	river-mouth	inner/inver	**Inner**leithen
tulach	knoll	tilli/tully	**Tilli**coultry

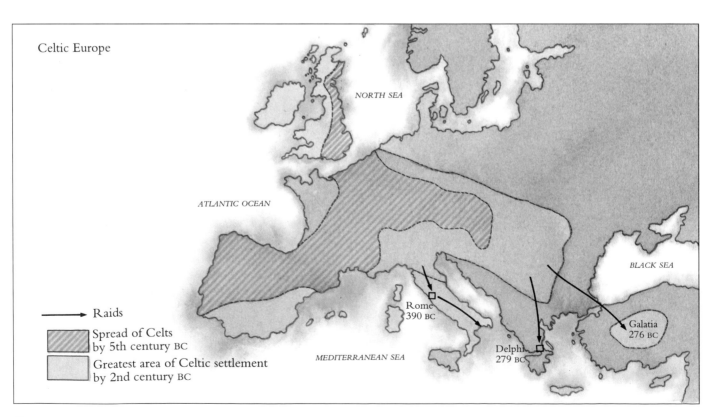

Celtic Europe

NORTH SEA

ATLANTIC OCEAN

BLACK SEA

Rome
390 BC

Galatia
276 BC

Delphi
279 BC

MEDITERRANEAN SEA

→ Raids

Spread of Celts by 5th century BC

Greatest area of Celtic settlement by 2nd century BC

From around AD 1100 onwards, some Lowland Scots began to speak more like the English and to copy their way of life. But elsewhere in Scotland, Celtic or Gaelic society continued to develop. Traditionally, large areas of the Highlands and the Islands were ruled by the Lord of the Isles with his Council. This sea-kingdom was patrolled by warriors in sleek galleys.

Many Lowlanders thought the Highland people were just rough and barbaric; but they were wrong. Life in the Highlands was harsh, but the Gaels admired people who were educated and artistic. Valuable skills were handed down through many generations. Members of a family often all learned the same profession, and became famous as a family of doctors, lawyers, poets, musicians, historians, stone and wood carvers, or metalsmiths. There were centres of learning and libraries of precious books throughout the Gaelic Highlands.

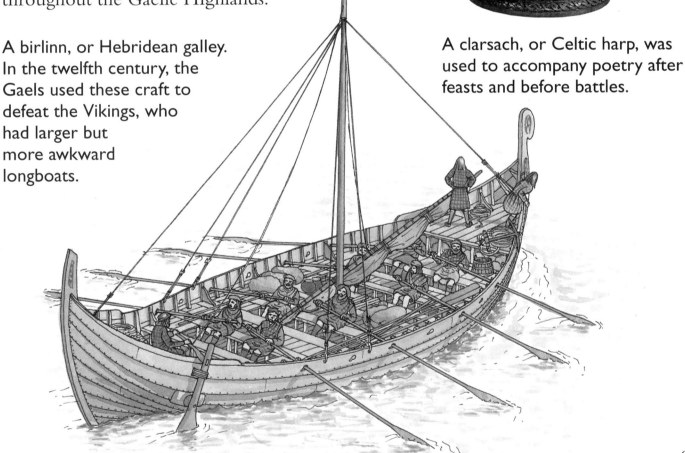

A birlinn, or Hebridean galley. In the twelfth century, the Gaels used these craft to defeat the Vikings, who had larger but more awkward longboats.

A clarsach, or Celtic harp, was used to accompany poetry after feasts and before battles.

A Divided Nation

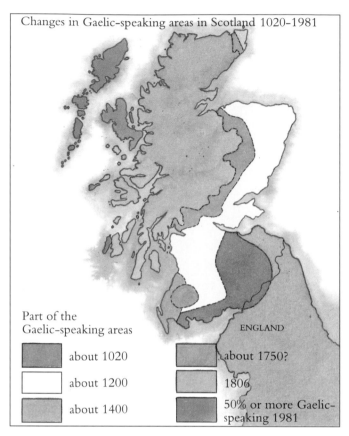

Changes in Gaelic-speaking areas in Scotland 1020–1981

ENGLAND

Part of the
Gaelic-speaking areas

about 1020	about 1750?
about 1200	1806
about 1400	50% or more Gaelic-speaking 1981

This map of Scotland shows how the Gaelic-speaking area has shrunk north-wards and westwards over the centuries.

The decline of the Gaelic language.

Two hundred and fifty years ago, one third of the population of Scotland lived in the Highlands. The islands and glens were bustling, lively places. If you had lived in the Highlands then, you would have spoken Gaelic yourself.

Over the years, Scotland became a divided nation. The Gaels and the Lowland English speakers did not trust each other. The Lowlanders looked down on the Highlanders, but they were also afraid of the fearsome military power of the Highland chiefs.

King James VI of Scotland showed little understanding of his Highland subjects when he said they were all barbarians:

'As for the Highlanders, I shortly comprehend them all in two sorts of people: the one that dwelleth in our mainland that are barbarous, and yet mixed with some show of civility; the other that dwelleth in the Isles and are all utterly barbarous.'

James VI of Scotland.

Highland chiefs led thousands of fierce warriors like these.

In the early seventeenth century, laws were passed to control the Gaels. Chiefs were forced to send their sons to be taught in English, in Lowland schools. This was part of a process that would change the Gaelic way of life. The Gaels were very sorry to see their language, Gaelic, lose its influence with important people. The Reverend John Maclean wrote:

'For a thousand years and more it held first place in the court of the kings, before the speech of the Southerners raised its head.'

(Translated from his poem in praise of Gaelic.)

Before the Clearances, most Scots lived in the Highlands and North East.

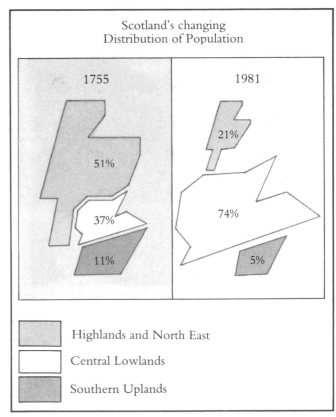

Scotland's changing Distribution of Population

1755

51%

37%

11%

1981

21%

74%

5%

Highlands and North East

Central Lowlands

Southern Uplands

11

What was a Clan?

The word 'clann' in Gaelic means 'children'. A Scottish clan was a group of people with close ties. Clan members often had the same surname and lived in the same area. Not all members of the clan were related, but they believed that they had a common ancestor.

The clan chief looked on his clan as a loyal 'family'. It was his duty to protect them, especially in times of hardship and famine. The clansmen always obeyed their chief. They were his own private army.

The chief controlled the clan lands. He divided and leased the farmland to tacksmen, who were often close relations. The tacksmen were the 'middle class' of the clan. They took charge of the day-to-day running of the land, and recruited the clansmen when they were needed to fight. The tacksmen rented the land to tenant farmers, who in turn employed cottars to work for them. The cottars helped in ploughing the fields, harvesting crops, herding cattle and cutting peat. In return they received a small patch of land on which to grow their own food.

Life was hard, but the Highlanders were devoted to their land. To them it was a land alive with stories and songs from clan history and legend.

The Highlanders drove cattle south to Lowland markets in the autumn.

The clansmen had two different ways of life. For part of the year they were farmers, growing crops and keeping cattle. In the fighting season (which was usually the summer), the men became warriors, following their chief into battle. Cattle-rustling (stealing) was part of their way of life. Traditions of clan honour, loyalty and duty were strong.

The clan system

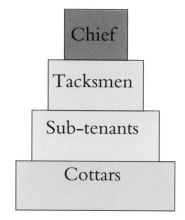

Castle Tioram, in Moidart. Chiefs lived in castles, which were usually well-placed for defence.

A Highland chieftain, about 1680. This is one of the earliest portraits showing Highland dress.

'Brosnachadh' is a kind of poetry that was written to encourage men before they went into battle:

> *Be vigorous, nimble-footed,*
> *In winning the battle*
> *Against your enemies*
> *O Children of Conn of the Hundred Battles*
> *Now is the time for you to win recognition.*
> *O battle-loving warriors,*
> *O brave, heroic firebrands*
> *The children of Conn of the Hundred Battles*
> *O Children of Conn remember*
> *Hardihood in time of battle.*

(Translated from Clan Donald's incitement to battle on the day of the Battle of Harlaw, 1411, by Lachlan Mòr MacMhuirich.)

Life in the Glens

Shielings: small stone houses. In summer, cattle were taken to the high pastures. Many township people moved with them for the season.

The Union with England

In 1603 Queen Elizabeth of England died. As she had no children to succeed her, her third cousin, James VI of Scotland, was asked by the English parliament to become king of England. He thus became James VI and I. This is known as the Union of the Crowns.

During the century after the Union of the Crowns, some people began to think it would be better if England and Scotland were joined into one country. Many Scots were unhappy at this idea. They were afraid that Scotland would not be an equal partner in the union, and some still wanted Scotland to have a separate monarch. As the argument went on, the people who were in favour of a union gained support, largely because of English threats and bribery. Many Scottish aristocrats accepted bribes in return for voting for a union.

Bribes accepted by Scottish aristocrats:	
Lord Elibank	£50
Earl of Findlater	£100
Lord Banff	£11 2s
Marquis of Montrose	£300
Lord Justice Clerk, Cockburn of Ormiston	£200
Earl of Balcarres	£500
Provost of Wigtown	£25
Lord High Commissioner	£12,325 10s

Source: Letters published in Memoirs of George Lockhart of Carnwath: Memoirs, 1817.

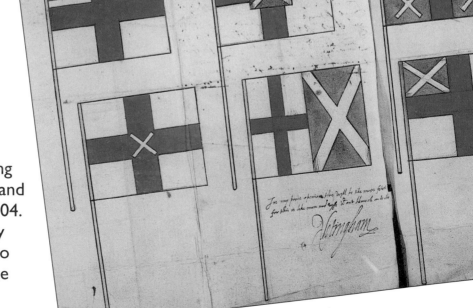

These ideas for joining the flags of Scotland and England are dated 1604. They show how early some people began to think of a union of the two nations.

Robert Burns 1759–1796, the famous Scottish poet, later wrote with contempt about the Treaty of Union and the way it was achieved:

Fareweel to a' our Scottish fame,
Fareweel our ancient glory!
Fareweel ev'n to the Scottish name,
Sae famed in martial story!
Now Sark rins over Solway sands
An' Tweed rins to the ocean,
To mark where England's province stands —
Such a parcel of rogues in a nation!
What force or guile could not subdue
Thro' many warlike ages
Is wrought now by a coward few
For hireling traitor's wages.
The English steel we could disdain,
Secure in valour's station;
But English gold has been our bane —
Such a parcel of rogues in a nation!

(From 'A Parcel of Rogues'.)

Andrew Fletcher, known as 'The Patriot' because of his loyalty to his country.

For hundreds of years, Scotland had been an independent nation with its own monarchy and parliament. In 1707 the Treaty of Union was signed, making England and Scotland one nation. Now a united parliament was to be based in London. An English government spy reported that the ordinary people of Scotland were 50 to 1 against the union, but they had no say in the matter. There were angry riots in Scotland's major cities. For the Highlanders, government was now further away than ever.

Andrew Fletcher of Saltoun, known as 'The Patriot', spoke out against the Union. He was afraid the Scots would be overruled by the English. He warned his fellow members of the Scottish Parliament in Edinburgh against a 'united parliament, where the English shall have so vast a majority . . . The Scots members may dance around to all eternity [forever] in the trap of their own making.' After the Union, Fletcher took no more part in politics, saying that Scotland was now 'fit only for the slaves who had sold it.'

The Jacobite Rebellions

King James VII and II was the fourth of the Stuarts, the Scottish royal family who ruled both Scotland and England. He was a Roman Catholic. His supporters were known as the Jacobites. In 1689 James was forced to give up his throne because the Scottish and English parliaments wanted a Protestant ruler. When he left, the throne was offered to his daughter Mary and her husband, Prince William of Orange.

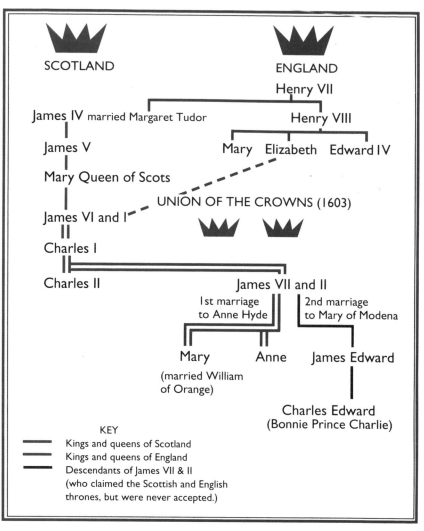

A family tree, showing how the Stuarts came to the English throne.

General Wade. Wade is famous for the roads he had built across Scotland to help keep control of the Highlands. A popular rhyme of the time said, 'If you had seen these roads before they were made, you would lift up your hands and bless General Wade.'

Most Jacobites felt that Scotland had been betrayed by the 1707 Treaty of Union. In 1715 and 1745 there were two major rebellions by the Jacobites, in which they tried to bring back the Stuarts as monarchs. The Stuarts made use of the loyalty of some Highland chiefs and the fierce bravery of their clansmen. Both rebellions failed. The rebellions became known as the 'Fifteen' and the 'Forty-five'.

David Morier's painting, A Jacobite Incident: Culloden. The 'Forty-five' rebellion was led by Charles Edward Stuart (often known as Bonnie Prince Charlie). The rebellion ended when the government army won the Battle of Culloden in April 1746.

After the 'Fifteen', General Wade was sent to keep the peace in the Highlands. He controlled the Highlanders by building forts in important places, and linking them with good roads. The third verse of the British National Anthem remembers General Wade:

'God grant that General Wade
May by Thy mighty aid
Victory bring
May he sedition hush
And like a torrent rush
Rebellious Scots to crush
God save the King.'

In London, the Gaels were seen as barbaric tribesmen who threatened England and the growth of the British Empire. After the 'Forty-five', many Jacobites were executed, imprisoned or banished. All of Gaelic Scotland was punished. Soldiers roamed the Highlands, carrying out brutal crimes against the people. New laws were passed, forbidding Highlanders to own weapons or to play the bagpipes. One of the worst things for the Gaels was being banned from wearing tartan and Highland dress (the kilt). Tartans had special meanings as symbols of clan loyalties. Clansmen felt shamed by wearing trousers. Chiefs lost their power to make law. The clan system was being destroyed.

The 'Forty-five'
- More Scots fought against Bonnie Prince Charlie than for him.
- At the Battle of Culloden, a third of the government army were Scots, and many Highlanders fought against the Jacobites.

Highland Life Changes

After 1745 things began to change a lot in Scotland. Many Scottish people moved into the growing factory towns in the Lowlands. In the past these people had grown their own food. Now, as town dwellers, they needed to buy food. Abroad, Britain was busy fighting long wars against France, and the British armies needed huge amounts of food. With this bigger market to sell to, landowners could now make large profits from farming their land more efficiently.

Throughout Scotland people were becoming interested in new ways of farming. This meant using crop rotation, land drainage, hardier animal breeds and new farm machines to grow more food and make more money. In the past, Highland landlords had shared the land with their clansfolk. Now they began to introduce some of the new farming ideas to make more money for themselves.

Landowners employed factors, or managers, to oversee the farm work. The tacksmen were no longer needed. Sheep walks were made by joining many small townships into large farms. Flocks of profitable sheep were reared on these.

Shepherds tending sheep on the Isle of Skye, on what had been township land.

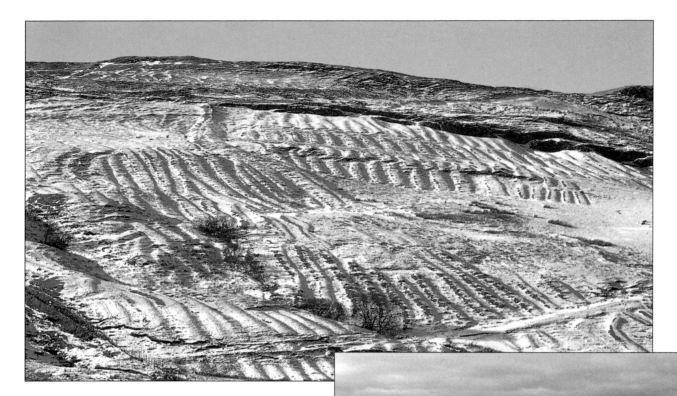

The shape of rigs (the old fields, divided up into strips) can still be seen clearly here in Glen Drynoch, on the Isle of Skye. Marks like these show the lines where crops were once grown.

Amongst the ruins of Rossal, a township that was cleared in Strathnaver. Until 1814, about 100 people lived there. Rossal was one of fifty settlements in the strath.

Sir John Sinclair of Ulbster had a plan to help his tenants stay on the land. They would hire a herdsman to look after a shared flock of about 300 sheep, and would pay part of the rent in wool and mutton. Unfortunately the plan was never tried. Like other lairds (landowners), he removed people who stood in the way of profit. Lairds no longer needed their clansmen as warriors. Instead they wanted farmers who would pay high cash rents.

The traditional life of the ordinary Highland people was being swept away. The small townships began to be destroyed and the people scattered.

The Clans are Scattered

From around 1760 onwards, more and more landowners in the north of Scotland brought sheep on to their estates. Many introduced a new breed of sheep, called the Cheviot. Cheviot sheep produced better, more valuable wool, than the smaller, native sheep. In winter the Cheviot needed to graze in the shelter of the valleys – where many people lived in townships. As a result, families were turned off their land and lost their homes. They were left with no way of feeding themselves.

Elizabeth Gordon, Countess of Sutherland, owned a huge estate in Scotland. Like many landowners, she usually lived in London and spoke no Gaelic. Her husband, George Leveson-Gower, was the Marquis of Stafford. When he inherited the wealth of his

uncle, their combined estates made them enormously wealthy. The income from the Staffords' estates brought them £300,000 each year. This would be worth many millions of pounds today.

Above:
The first Duke of Sutherland.

Left:
Dunrobin Castle, Golspie, was the home of the Countess and Duke of Sutherland.

A poor Highlander's home
on the Isle of Skye, 1853.

The Staffords owned two-thirds of the land in Sutherland. Their letters show that they both took an active interest in 'improving' their Scottish estates. They drew up plans to:

- take power away from the tacksmen.
- end the runrig system (the old division of fields into strips. Each tenant had a number of strips for growing crops).
- turn many small farms into large farms, to be rented to southern sheep farmers.
- move the original Highlanders to the coast where they could take up other work.

The Marquess of Stafford became the first Duke of Sutherland, and he is remembered as a 'Great Improver'. Yet even today, many people feel bitter that the 'improvements' forced on the people did not make life better for everyone.

This record, showing some of the removals from the Sutherland estate, dates from 1819.

The Sutherland Clearances

James Loch was the factor who ran the Staffords' estates. He did not like Gaels, believing they were lazy and dirty. He cleared the main glens in Sutherland where many people lived. He wanted to change the way the people lived, and to get more money from rents for his employers.

The Highlanders were not given a choice about Loch's changes. Promises to resettle them properly were not always kept. At least 10,000 people were evicted (turned out) from their homes between 1807 and 1821 – which was almost half the population of Sutherland. The Loch Policy was hated by most Gaels.

Patrick Sellar, a lawyer, was employed by the Countess of Sutherland to collect rents, keep accounts and make sure the tenants obeyed estate rules. Like Loch, Sellar looked down on the Gaels. He is bitterly remembered in a Gaelic poem written by Donald Baillie in 1816, called 'The Black Tinker'. Here is one verse from it:

Tha Sellar an Cuil-mhàillidh
Air fhàgail mar mhadadh-allaidh
A' glacadh is a'sàradh
Gach aon ni a thig na charaibh
(Gaelic)

Sellar is in Culmaily
Left there like a wolf
Seizing and oppressing
All that comes within his reach
(English translation)

Map labels:
ATLANTIC OCEAN
Strathnaver
Badinloskin
Armadale
Farr
Loch Naver
Helmsdale
Strath of Kildonan
Brora
Dunrobin Castle
Lairg
Golspie
Culmaily
Dornoch
MORAY FIRTH
N S E W

Grace Macdonald, who was a young girl of nineteen at the time, later recalled:

'There was no mercy or pity shown to young or old. All had to clear away, and those who could not get their effects [belongings] removed in time to a safe distance had them burnt before their eyes. They were happy in Strathnaver, with plenty to take and give, but all are very poor now.'
(Napier Commission of Inquiry, 1883.)

Patrick Sellar's first farm 1814
Extent of the Sutherland estates 1814

In 1814, remembered as the Year of the Burnings, Sellar evicted tenants in Strathnaver. He gave orders to burn the hill grazing areas so there would be no food for the tenants' cattle and the people would have to go. Buildings were burned to stop the people staying on the land.

Donald MacLeod, a Gael, wrote:

'I was present at the pulling down and burning of the house of William Chisholm, (of) Badinloskin, in which was lying his wife's mother, an old bedridden woman of near 100 years of age. . . I told him (Sellar) of the poor old woman. . . He replied, "Damn her, the old witch; she has lived too long. Let her burn!". . . She died within five days.'

(From *Gloomy Memories*, Donald MacLeod, 1857.)

Patrick Sellar, later in life.

Patrick Sellar

A lawyer and 'improver'. In 1816 Sellar stood trial for murder and fire-raising. The jury found him not guilty. After the trial, Loch wrote to the Countess of Sutherland that Sellar was 'really guilty of many very oppressive acts'. Sellar went on to become a rich landowner.

Patrick Sellar watches the burning of William Chisholm's house, witnessed by Donald MacLeod.

Why was there no Revolution?

Strathcarron, 1854 - the surname of some of the victims has given this incident the name: 'the Massacre of the Rosses'.

Although the Gaels were treated so badly, there was no full-scale revolution. There are many explanations for this. The Highlanders were forbidden to own weapons after the 'Forty-five', so they had nothing to fight with. Also, they remembered the cruelty of the government soldiers after the 'Forty-five', and this made them afraid to disturb the peace.

To help them carry out evictions, some landowners used soldiers. In several places police charged with their batons at people who did try to resist eviction. In Strathcarron in Ross-shire in 1854, police beat and kicked the women of Gruinards (pronounced Greenyards). Donald Ross, a lawyer and journalist from Glasgow, was shown the women's clothing after the attack. In a letter to the Lord Advocate of Scotland, Ross described the clothes as being: 'completely dyed red with their blood. There were caps with holes in them where the batons tore and carried the thin cotton with them into the skulls. . .'

Many Gaels had lost their leaders. They were loyal to the old way of life and would not disobey their chief, the father of the clan. They were not ready to admit that their chiefs had abandoned them for money.

The Church also failed to support the Gaels. The Highlanders, who were very religious people, looked to their church ministers for help. But landowners were often responsible for appointing the minister to the local church, so these ministers did and said what the landowners wanted. They told the people not to break the law.

Other ministers were unhappy about the landowners' control of the Church. In 1843 they left the Church of Scotland in protest, and formed the Free Church, leaving the old parish churches empty.

Although the Church offered little help, some people still went to their former place of worship for refuge. In 1845, the people who used to worship in Croick Church returned to camp in the churchyard after they were evicted. They scratched sad messages on the windows.

A reporter from the *Times* newspaper described the scene:

'A fire was kindled in the churchyard round which the poor children clustered. Two cradles with infants in them were placed close to the fire, and sheltered round by the dejected–looking mothers.'

Above:
Croick Church,
Strathcarron,
Ross-shire.

Left:
A family being
evicted from
their home.

Emigration and Famine

Thomas Faed's painting *The Last of the Clan*. It is meant to show the sadness of Highlanders saying goodbye to family and friends.

During the period 1762–1886, hundreds of Clearances took place – from Shetland to Arran, and from Aberdeenshire to the Western Isles. Whether or not they had actually been evicted from their homes, many people left the country in the hope of a better life elsewhere. Many went by ship on long voyages. For the poorer passengers, emigration was a desperate journey during which many died. During the century of the Clearances, about 100,000 people left the Highlands for the New World.

To get more fares, emigration agents took on too many passengers. Often, ships were kept waiting in the harbour until the emigrants' own food was gone, and then they were overcharged for new supplies. People were crammed together in filthy spaces between the decks, sometimes for as long as three months. Diseases such as cholera, smallpox, dysentery and typhoid were common.

In spite of the Clearances, however, the population of the Highlands was still increasing dramatically. Between 1801 and 1821, the population of Inverness-shire increased by 24 per cent, and that of Argyll by 20 per cent. This meant that more people were crowded on to less land, and were in even greater danger from hunger and disease.

The potato was the main crop grown by the Highlanders. In 1846 a potato disease called 'blight' ruined most of the harvest. Mass starvation was only avoided by government help, charity from the south and the efforts of some landowners.

A new Poor Law, passed in 1845, ruled that landlords had to take care of the poor on their land. The famine in 1846 helped to convince landlords that they should evict people rather than pay to support them.

The government, charitable societies and some landlords organized emigration and paid many of the emigrants' fares. One charity, the Highland and Island Emigration Society, raised money to pay for more than 10,000 people to go to Canada, and almost 4,000 to go to Australia.

Inverness Courier 28 May 1845

EMIGRATION
At Glasgow for New York
By American Passenger Packet Ship
Warsaw
600 tons burthen
N.T. Hawkins, Commander
who is well known in the trade for his care and attention to passengers, will be ready to receive goods in a few days, and be despatched positively on 15 June.
This fine vessel has great height between Decks, and in every respect suitable and superior accommodation for Cabin, Intermediate and Steerage Passengers, as she will be fitted up on the most approved principle, according to Act of Parliament, and Emigrants may rely on every attention being paid to their health and comfort. Immediate application is recommended.
For freight or passage, apply to:
C.J. Bancks, 130 Broomielaw.
N.B. The usual allowances of Bread and Potatoes; Tea, Sugar, Tobacco &c free of Duty.
Glasgow 22 May 1845

An emigration advert. Shipping agents tried to reassure emigrants that conditions on board would be good.

The *Hercules* in the harbour at Campbeltown with emigrants from the Isle of Skye, in January 1853.

Where did the People Go?

Those who left the Highlands did one of four things. They moved to the coast, to the Lowlands, to join the armed forces or they went abroad.

THE COAST

Some people who were evicted settled on the coast on new crofts (small farms). The crofts were often on rocky, infertile ground, and were too small to feed a family properly and pay the rent. Landowners raised the rent if the crofters did anything to make their land better. Many of these poor sites were abandoned in later years.

A few landowners planned new villages and jobs on the coast, but there was never enough work for everyone. Traditionally the people lived by farming. Some people did learn new skills and faced the dangerous seas to earn a living.

INVERNESS COURIER
9 September 1829

HERRING FISHING – SIX MEN DROWNED

On the evening of Monday 24 August, the fishing boats at Wick went out as usual in quest of herring. During the night a very strong breeze sprang up from the north-west, which scattered most of the boats up and down the firth; and lamentable to relate, one of the boats, belonging to Pulteney, has not been heard of since.

All hope of her return has been given up, as the crew of a south firth boat, during the gale, came in contact with a boat with her keel uppermost, and, getting entangled in her drift of nets, was in danger of sharing the same fate, having to unship their rudder to get free of her nets.

There were five men on board; two of them have left families – one with three and the other with four children. On the same night (Monday) as the boats were going out of the bay, one man was thrown overboard by a sweep of the sail and drowned – his body has not yet been found.

This newspaper article tells of the many dangers which faced those who went fishing.

A memorial by the ruins at Badbea Crofts - a clifftop site that was abandoned in 1911. Families that lived there had to tether their little children, to stop them falling over the cliff edge.

Kelpers on the Isle of Skye. Many people worked up to their waists in water cutting the seaweed.

But fishing was not a reliable way of earning a living. In the north-east the fishing failed when the shoals of herring, the most important fish, moved away.

At first large numbers of people found work on the western coast and islands gathering seaweed. The seaweed, called kelp, was burnt to a powder and used in making soap, glass and fertilizer. The landlords who owned the kelp made a lot of money. It suited them to keep a large population as a source of cheap labour. As many people had little or no land, they had to gather kelp to make a living. However, after 1811 the price of kelp fell, and over the next twenty years the kelp industry became less profitable than sheep farming. Once again, cottars and crofters were cleared.

The poet John MacLean of Tiree wrote of the crofters:

'A few remain on headlands of the sea,
Driven to the shore and flayed with rents.'

A typical coastal settlement site.

THE LOWLANDS

After the evictions began, many families moved to the cities to escape from poverty. They went to cities like Glasgow, where there was work to be found in textile mills, on the railways, in the coal mines and building ships. The cities grew so quickly that it was impossible to build decent homes fast enough. Conditions in the three- and four-storey tenements were very bad.

Growth in Glasgow's population			
1780	1811	1841	1871
42,000	100,700	274,000	477,700

The immigrant areas were the poorest in the cities. There was little sanitation (drainage and sewage), no proper water supply and rubbish lay in the street. Two or three families often had to share one or two rooms. Rents were not always cheap, and people were put out on the street if they could not pay the rent on time.

Slum housing in Glasgow, 1868.

A shipyard on the Clyde, 1878. Many Highlanders found work on the River Clyde.

New Lanark, founded by David Dale in 1785, was a model of good working and living conditions.

In the overcrowded and dirty conditions, disease was a real danger. Infectious diseases like cholera, typhus and smallpox killed many people.

The refugees found some support in the Gaelic Clubs and Highland Societies set up by earlier immigrants. There were also Gaelic chapels in many towns and cities. In Glasgow in the early 1830s, it is thought there were more than 5,000 children under the age of ten who spoke Gaelic as their first language.

Working conditions in the mills and factories were usually hard. Children were employed and worked long hours. At New Lanark, the mill owners, David Dale and Robert Owen, tried to make the lives of their workers as comfortable as possible. They built good houses, which are still in use today. They tried to employ Highlanders in the mills. Every Highlander who came to New Lanark was given a house at a low rent and a secure job. For these people, the move to the south was more successful.

Robert Owen. Owen proved it was possible to treat employees well, and make a profit.

33

THE ARMED FORCES

Even before the Clearances, a few Highland regiments were raised. The clan chiefs later made up many more regiments using their tenants. They did this to get money or favours from the government in London. The chiefs appealed to feelings of clan loyalty. They also often threatened tenants with eviction, and many young men joined the regiments in the belief that they would be saving their parents from eviction.

Until the ban on Highland dress ended in 1782, only members of the British Army could legally wear it. Pride in the kilt encouraged Highland men to become recruits. The townships of the Scottish Highlands were emptied of tens of thousands of men to fight Britain's foreign wars.

Major General James Wolfe saw the Highlanders fight at the Battle of Culloden and was impressed. He wanted Highlanders to help fight the French in North America. He wrote:

'They are hardy, intrepid [fearless], accustomed to rough country and no great mischief if they fall [die]. How can you better employ a secret enemy than by making his end conducive to [work for] the common good?'

(from Wolfe's letter to his friend, William Rickson.)

Major General Wolfe, leading a successful attack on Quebec, Canada, 1759. Half the British killed in the fighting were Highlanders.

Despite his wounds, this piper bravely plays to encourage his comrades to victory against the French at the Battle of Vimeiro, 1808.

Highland regiments

● Between 1793 and 1815, 72,385 Highlanders served in the British Army.
● In 1854, the government had difficulty getting Highland recruits for the war against Russia in the Crimea. Evictions had emptied the old recruiting areas. The chiefs' influence had gone. Angry Highlanders protested by making noises like sheep and dogs at recruiting meetings. In Sutherland, the men said:

> 'We have no country to fight for. You robbed us of our country and gave it to the sheep. Therefore, since you have preferred sheep to men, let sheep defend you.'

(From *The Northern Ensign*, Donald Ross.)

Usually, Highlanders were the best-disciplined soldiers in the British Army. They felt responsible for each other and for their relatives at home. Even Britain's enemies, like Emperor Napoleon of France, admired their bravery. However, when the army authorities broke promises they had made to Highland regiments, or insulted the Highlanders' sense of honour, there were serious mutinies - sixteen by 1804.

ABROAD

'Many of the people here have emigrated to America: many more are preparing to go to Australia. In some parts of this parish, where there was dense population 80 years ago, there are now to be found only a few scattered huts.'
(The New Statistical Account, Laggan, Inverness-shire, 1835.)

During the eighteenth and nineteenth centuries, thousands of Highlanders went abroad to find a better life for themselves and their families. They went all over the world (see map below), especially to the 'new' countries to which people were encouraged to go and settle on the land. The Scottish influence can be seen on any map of these countries – many towns, rivers and mountains have Scottish names.

Highland culture has spread all over the world, and can be seen in Highland Gatherings, pipe bands and the wearing of the kilt. This piper is in Virginia, USA.

CANADA

SCOTLAND

USA

SOUTH AFRICA

AUSTRALIA

NEW ZEALAND

A map of the world, showing where the emigrants from Scotland went.

This illustration from 1878 shows emigrants building a new life for themselves in Canada.

The gravestone of an emigrant, Prince Edward Island, Canada. Thousands left Scotland for the New World, never to return home.

Those who emigrated often followed friends and relatives who had gone before. They received letters encouraging them to leave their Highland homes. Sometimes whole communities sailed together to build a new life overseas.

Some landlords, like the Earl of Selkirk, tried to help these settlers. After the clearances in Sutherland, Selkirk took a shipload of people to his colony at Red River in Canada. Life there was hard: people had to clear their own farmland. The people who already lived there were not always friendly, and food and tools were scarce.

The Highlanders who emigrated carried their traditions of loyalty, duty, religion and education with them. They added a great deal to the life of their new countries.

Notable Gaels

Alexander Mackenzie was born on the Isle of Lewis. He emigrated to Canada, where he explored large areas of the country. The Mackenzie River was named after him.

John A. Macdonald emigrated to Canada as a boy. He worked to bring the provinces of Canada together, and became the first prime minister of the Dominion of Canada.

Lachlan Macquarie was born on the Island of Ulva, near Mull. He had a long military career before becoming governor of New South Wales in Australia in 1808.

The Crofters' War

Carl Haag's water-colour painting *Morning in the Highlands* shows Queen Victoria and her royal party. She made the Highlands a fashionable place for the wealthy to visit.

By the 1850s, cheaper wool imported from abroad was making sheep farms in the Highlands less profitable. So instead of sheep farming, landowners began to set up sporting estates and to clear the land for deer-stalking. When Queen Victoria built her royal castle at Balmoral in 1855, tourism in the Highlands increased. Railways and steamships brought people to enjoy shooting and fishing in the emptied land. The Highlands and Islands became a holiday playground for the rich. Few appreciated the distress of the natives.

Protesting crofters confront the law on the Isle of Lewis. (From the *Illustrated London News*, 1888.)

Desperate to keep the little they still had, in the 1880s the Highland crofters rose up against the landowners. Thousands joined Land Leagues to campaign for changes in the land laws.

The crofters had strong, popular leaders. They were helped by Gaels who lived outside the Highlands, and by outspoken church ministers. The crofters wanted to protect the Highland traditions and culture. They argued that more Gaelic should be taught. The movement published its own magazines, and managed to get supporters elected as Members of Parliament.

'We labour to form an opinion in this country in favour of the restoration of the land to the people. . .'
(From *The Highlander,* editorial by John Murdoch, 23 March 1881.)

Men and women fought in violent clashes with police. Gunboats arrived with soldiers to keep the peace, but nothing stopped the crofters' campaign.

'Your fathers kept quiet – quiet since the '45. Tell me what they gained by it? Still keep up your agitation; let your enemies see you are not afraid of police or military – your agitation must and will go on until your wrongs are righted.'
(Ronald MacLean, speaking on the Isle of Skye, 1884)

In 1883 the government gave Lord Napier the job of finding out why there was trouble in the Highlands. He questioned many people and wrote a report. In 1886, the Crofter Act was passed which protected crofters from eviction and unfair rents. The *Oban Times* called it an 'instalment of justice', but the Act did not return the land to the people. For thirty years disturbances continued. Crofters made land raids to try and take back a few small areas of land.

John McPherson, a crofters' leader, speaks at a meeting on the Isle of Skye. (From the *Illustrated London News,* 1884.)

The Highlands Today

Deer grazing on land where crofters once grew crops, on the Isle of Rum, now a National Nature Reserve.

Most of the Highlands still lies empty in the hands of a tiny number of landowners. Crofting communities have shrunk and still struggle to survive. Young people have had to leave the Highlands to find jobs.

Today, new groups of people want to have a say on how the land should be used. They are interested in nature conservation, outdoor leisure, tourism and business. People now realize that everyone's activities have to be managed in a balanced way to avoid damaging the environment. Some people think that government money should be used to buy land suitable for conservation.

Many people think the Highlands are a natural wilderness. In fact the landscape has been damaged over many centuries. Since the Clearances, using the land to graze sheep and deer has ruined its natural cover. Sheep eat the best grass. They cause coarser plants to spread. Grazing too many deer and sheep has also stopped young trees from growing. Another practice that has damaged the land is the burning of hill land every few years. This is meant to help new grass and plants to grow in spring, but it is often overdone. After the burning, rain can wash the goodness from the soil, so that plants actually grow less well.

The old traditions of crofting for crops and cattle are now seen as being better for the environment. They do little harm to wildlife or plants, and they give work to people. Crofters in Assynt, Sutherland recently joined together and bought land with public support. But crofters are not as wealthy as the many outsiders who buy estates in the Highlands.

The Clearances have never been forgotten. Neither has the Highlanders' dream of having, once again, 'the land for the people'.

'The tears come close to my eyes when I think of all we suffered, and of the sorrows, hardships and oppression we came through. I pray that our present struggles will soon be over, that our children will have plenty of the land that is in the big farms for their homes and enjoy the fruits of the land as we did in those faraway days, without fear and without oppression. The Earth is the Lord's and the fullness thereof. The Earth He has given to the children of men.'
(Peggy MacCormack, quoted in Alexander Carmichael's folklore collection *Carmina Gadelica*, 1900.)

Muirburn (the burning of hill land) in progress.

Crofting today in the township of Staffin, Isle of Skye.

Glossary

Cottars
The farm hands and families who worked the land for the tenant farmers.

Crofts
Small farms of a few acres of land. People who work crofts are called crofters.

Crop rotation
A system of farming in which the crop that is grown in a field is changed from year to year, to keep the soil healthy.

Emigration
Leaving your home country.

Eviction
The forcible moving of people, by law, out of houses and off the land.

Factor
The word used in Scotland for an estate manager.

Gaelic
The language of the Gaels. Gaelic is still spoken in Scotland and abroad.

Gaels
One of the Celtic family of peoples. They settled in, Scotland, Ireland, and the Isle of Man, and were the original Scots.

Jacobites
Supporters of the Stuarts, the Scottish royal family. The word Jacobite comes from the Latin word for James, 'Jacobus', which King James VII and II used when he signed documents.

Laird
A lord or landowner.

Monarch
The king or queen of a country.

Mutinies
Uprisings against authority, usually in the armed forces.

Runrig
The old Scottish system of dividing the land for crops into strips. Each year the rigs were shared among the tenants in a township, giving each farmer a share of good and poor land.

Sheep walks
Large sheep farms, made by joining the old, small townships together.

Tacksmen
The men who leased out land for their chiefs to the tenant farmers. They were responsible for collecting rents and sharing out the land.